THE BAR ROOM

LONGFELLOW'S
WAYSIDE INN

A CAMERA IMPRESSION

by SAMUEL CHAMBERLAIN

HASTINGS HOUSE *Publishers* NEW YORK

FOREWORD

AMERICAN antiquity has no more eloquent spokesman than the gracious old Inn which, for over two centuries, has extended its hospitality to the traveler along the stagecoach highway (now Route 20) at South Sudbury, Massachusetts, some twenty miles west of Boston. Today, as in the 17th century, it is still maintained as an inn, to be enjoyed by a vastly greater number of visitors than in the stagecoach days. The atmosphere of age and tranquillity which delighted Longfellow has changed not a particle, although it is no longer a "rambling, tumble-down old building," as the poet found it in 1862. The "winding road, shaded by grand old oaks" is still there; so is the barn, and the brook and the stone bridge mentioned by him. Longfellow's affection for the Inn may have dated from his youth, when he took a stagecoach trip to Albany. South Sudbury was then a logical stop-over for the first night out of Boston. In later years he made several trips to the Inn, but whether he met there with some of the characters mentioned in the "Tales of a Wayside Inn" is uncertain. Four of these, however, Thomas W. Parsons (the Poet), Daniel Treadwell (the Theologian), Luigi Monti (the Sicilian), and Henry Ware Wales (the Student) were frequent visitors. The identity of the Inn was indicated so clearly in Longfellow's immensely popular poem that, after its publication in 1863, the old place became known as The Wayside Inn.

3

Previous to this time it had enjoyed a colorful history. The Howes of Sudbury, who built the Inn and maintained it from father to son for 174 years, were a long-lived lot. John Howe, sometimes called the "immigrant ancestor" of the Wayside Inn, came to this country from England in 1638 and settled in Sudbury. His son, Samuel Howe, a carpenter by trade, built the house which is the present Inn building in 1686, and opened it as a place of public entertainment. David Howe, Samuel's son, was the innkeeper of Howe's Tavern, as it was then called, from 1710 to 1746. Ezekiel Howe, David's son, was the third landlord for the half century between 1746 and 1796. He changed the name to the "Red Horse Tavern," and hung out the sign which is still in place. The device of the red horse painted on the sign was a help to travelers who could not read, but could easily recognize the red silhouette. Ezekiel Howe was an active patriot, and during the Revolutionary War led a company of Sudbury men at North Bridge in Concord. The fourth Howe landlord was Adam (1796-1830), and the fifth was his son, Lyman Howe, who held the reins from 1830 until he died in 1860. Lyman Howe was a bachelor, and at his death the furnishings were sold at auction. The house, however, was kept in the possession of the Howe heirs, though not licensed as an inn, until 1896, when it was bought by Mr. Edward R. Lemon, who effected many repairs and reopened it as an inn. In 1923 it was purchased from Mrs. Lemon by Mr. Henry Ford, who is maintaining the old tradition and keeping it open to travelers. Mr. Ford has retraced many of the Howe furnishings and has brought them back to the Inn, and has furnished the rooms so carefully that the ancient atmosphere has been preserved with gratifying accuracy. Not only the Inn building but the smaller houses on the 5000-acre estate, the farm buildings, the schools and the incomparable countryside have been preserved as they were in less hurried centuries.

This little book exhibits a certain temerity in aspiring to capture, by means of photographs taken in all seasons of the year, some part of the hospitable charm, the tranquillity, the beauty of countryside which the Wayside Inn has reflected since it was

> *"Built in the old Colonial day,*
> *When men lived in a grander way*
> *With ampler hospitality."*

1683

Longfellow's
Wayside
Inn
To The Right

WORCESTER
—
WAYSIDE
INN

SIGN AT THE
CROSSROADS

5

Four Seasons at the Wayside Inn

Winter

Spring

Summer

3

Autumn

"And, half effaced by rain and shine,
The Red Horse prances on the sign."

Through this hospitable front door travelers have passed for more than 250 years to find, beyond the threshold, a warm welcome in the noble old rooms of the Inn. The years have wrought surprisingly little change in the interior of the Inn, which now welcomes you. . . .

THE
STAIR RAIL

18

The gracious old room which first welcomes the visitor was once the bar room *(see frontispiece)* of the Inn. In the center is a hutch table dating from about 1650 (hutch meaning hiding place). The top unlocks and tips back, revealing a box for valuables and linen. The old high-backed settle is from the late 17th century. Over the fireplace is a Revolutionary musket, carried by a Sudbury man, Ephriam Smith. He was allowed the gun by the town authorities. The receipt promising its safe return was signed by Smith, April 17, 1775, and is still preserved in this room. Two original Paul Revere prints hang on the wall. The fireplace wall is further enlivened by a powder horn and canteen, pipe tongs, a wafer iron bearing the seal of the United States, and a rarity, a warming pan with an iron handle. There is also a pipe box, with a tobacco drawer, once filled with clay pipes. These long-stemmed pipes had their sanitary advantages, since the ends could be broken off when a new smoker used the pipe.

THE BAR ROOM   *(below)* THE PARLOR

"And in the parlor, full in view,
His coat-of-arms, well framed and glazed,
Upon the wall in colors blazed;"

THE PARLOR *(opposite bottom)*

This is the setting for Longfellow's "Tales of a Wayside Inn." The poet pictured his friends grouped about this fireplace—the poet, the student, the theologian, the Sicilian, the landlord and the Spanish Jew. Their photographs now appear on the far wall. The celebrated Ole Bull was the musician. Over the mantel is the Howe coat-of-arms and the panes of glass containing the name and the inscription of Major Molineaux, described by the poet. Pewter whale-oil lamps and authentically old sconces enrich the mantel wall. The fender is unusually delicate. Some of the Inn's finest antique hooked rugs are found in this parlor. They are colored by vegetable dyes, and possessed of astounding wearing qualities.

THE WASHINGTON ROOM

This room is named in honor of George Washington, who visited the Inn during Revolutionary days. There is no definite record that Washington spent the night here, but he stopped to greet Ezekiel Howe, the Inn's fighting landlord.

The old field bed is covered with a hand-made netted canopy. A handsome Windsor comb back chair sits in the corner. On the mantel shelf is an iron rush holder. On the table between the windows is an old Bible box with a pen and ink compartment. This contains the Howe family Bible with the family records. The old wooden cradle *(opposite)* dates from about 1700.

THE DINING ROOM
This was formerly the carriage shed, under the ballroom, and its conversion into a dining room is comparatively recent.

THE LOWER HALL *(opposite)*
The handsome staircase dates from about 1800, when the ballroom wing was built.

THE OLD KITCHEN

Here the meals were prepared for the traveler before an open fire, and even today "Old Kitchen Dinners" are served in this room. A red checkered tablecloth then covers the table and the cook, in costume, does her work exclusively at the fireplace. Originally this was a living room as well as a kitchen, and many household arts were practiced here. Besides the spinning wheel in the corner there is a pewter candle mould in wooden frame, capable of making two dozen candles at a time, a huge wooden bowl carved from one piece, and used for working buttermilk out of butter. There is much fine pewter on the old 17th century pine dresser. Adjoining the fireplace is a high-backed, "no-draft" bench for chilly nights. On the mantel is an old brass clock jack. This turned the roasting spit and saved a small boy for other tasks.

AMONG THE FITTINGS OF THE OLD KITCHEN FIREPLACE ARE THE BRASS
CLOCK JACK, A PISTOL TINDER, BETTY AND PHOEBE LAMPS, TOASTERS,
TRIVETS, SPIDERS, AND A COAL CARRIER TO TRANSPORT LIVE COALS.

A CORNER OF THE
LAFAYETTE ROOM
WHICH THE GREAT
GENERAL OCCUPIED
WHEN HE VISITED
THE WAYSIDE INN
IN 1824

THE OLD DINING ROOM

It looks small now, but in the early days this room was large enough for the limited number of stagecoach guests who paused for a meal. The 17th century hutch table of curly maple is surrounded by old braced-back Windsor chairs. The table is set with pewter dishes and porringers, and two-pronged forks. The caster for salt belonged to the Howe family. On the left wall is a blue-green spoon rack holding moulded pewter spoons. The woodwork is painted a delightful and undefinable shade of green. The floorboards in this room are very old, and some of them attain surprising width.

THE PARSONS ROOM   *(below)* THE LONGFELLOW ROOM

The Edison Room is named in honor of the great inventor, who was a visitor to the Wayside Inn, and slept in this room. The furniture is from the period of Mr. Edison's childhood.

The Parsons Room *(top, opposite)* is named in honor of Thomas W. Parsons, who was the poet in the "Tales of a Wayside Inn." A famed translator of Dante, Parsons was given the key to Florence in recognition of his work. Under the canopied field bed is a trundle bed for children.

The Longfellow Room *(bottom, opposite)* is named as a memorial to the poet, who was an occasional visitor to the Inn. The room contains another distinguished mantel, this time embellished with a Franklin stove.

35170

The Old Ballroom, built about 1800, has a handsome vaulted ceiling, blackened in the middle to conceal the smudge of the candles in the chandeliers. Around the walls are seats which open up to receive the wraps of the guests. At one end is a raised platform for the fiddlers. Humorous old English prints brighten the walls.

THE OLD BALLROOM

THE COACH HOUSE

Facing the old Post Road is this picturesque structure, built from old timbers in 1909. It now contains two historic stagecoaches. One of them is the Governor Eustis Coach, in which Lafayette rode to the laying of the cornerstone of Bunker Hill Monument in 1824. The other is the Bear Camp River Coach, which plied between Ossipee and Union, New Hampshire.

THE COACH HOUSE

ROSES
FRAME
THE
GARDEN
GATE

3

THE SAME SPOT IN THE GARDEN — IN SUMMER AND WINTER

THE GARDEN IN MIDSUMMER

A BUST OF THE POET GRACES THE BRICK GARDEN WALL *(opposite)*

THE POND — IN SPRING AND SUMMER

The Pond, sometime known as Josephine pond, reflects many a sylvan setting. It serves as a skating pond in winter and provides ice for the Inn.

THE OLD BARN

"Across the road the barns display
Their lines of stalls, their mows of hay"

In the old barn are two noteworthy vehicles of other days. One is the Marlboro-Northboro-Shrewsbury-Worcester Coach, made by the celebrated firm of Abbott and Downing in Concord, New Hampshire. The other is an old sleigh Coach.

THE BARN — IN SPRINGTIME AND IN WINTER

MID-
SUMMER
SIL-
HOUETTE

46

INTERIORS OF THE BARN

PURE AMERICAN COUNTRYSIDE

THE WILLOWS   *(below)* THE BROOK

**THE
OLD
STONE
BRIDGE**

*"And, leaning o'er the bridge of stone,
To watch the speckled trout glide by,"*

THE WAYSIDE INN AS SEEN FROM THE REDSTONE SCHOOL

The Redstone School *(opposite)* — Built in Sterling, Mass. in 1798, this is the little red schoolhouse attended by Mary Sawyer, who was Mary in the classic poem of "Mary Had a Little Lamb." It served as a school for about 60 years, and when purchased by Mr. Ford it was being used as a garage. The building was brought to the Wayside Inn estate in 1927, and now incorporates the original school, with the old key still locking the door. The bell which called Mary to school, and the chair in which sat Polly Kimball, the teacher, all exist in place. Sixteen Sudbury children from the first four grades attend the school regularly and sit at old desks their great-grandmothers might have used.

THE GAMBRELLED COTTAGE   *(below)* THE GRIST MILL

54

The Grist Mill, a typical 18th century mill with overshot water wheel, was built on an old mill site with stone taken from the Wayside Inn property. Here is ground the flour which is used for the Inn and the schools. Some sixteen kinds of unbleached flour and cereal are ground here by the old-fashioned method which preserves the germ of the wheat. Cracked wheat for breakfast cereal and a very fine water-ground corn meal used for making Indian pudding are among its many products. Old French Burr stones, found on the battlefields of France, are used for the grinding.

THE MILL STREAM — IN WINTER AND FALL

WINTRY SILHOUETTE   (below) MILLSTONES IN THE FIELDS

THE
RACEWAY

61

THE PARMENTER SISTERS HOUSE AND *(below)* ITS HUGE CHIMNEY

The nearby Calvin Howe House (18th century) now contains classrooms and dormitories for the Wayside Inn Boys School. Here fifty boys receive a high school education as well as agricultural training on the Wayside Inn estate. In the rear is an athletic field and tennis court space. This school was opened in 1928.

THE CALVIN HOWE POND

The General Store *(opposite)* — an old country store originally built in Sudbury Center and moved to the Wayside Inn property in 1929.

MIDSUMMER CLOUDS
OVER THE WAYSIDE INN

THE ADAM HOWE HOUSE

**THE ADAM
HOWE HOUSE**

THE ADAM HOWE BARN   *(below)* THE OLD WALKER HOUSE

NOBSCOT COTTAGE
This old gambrelled homestead rests under the shadow of Mt. Nobscot on
the Wayside Inn estate.

NOBSCOT COTTAGE   *(below and opposite)* THE SOUTHWEST SCHOOL

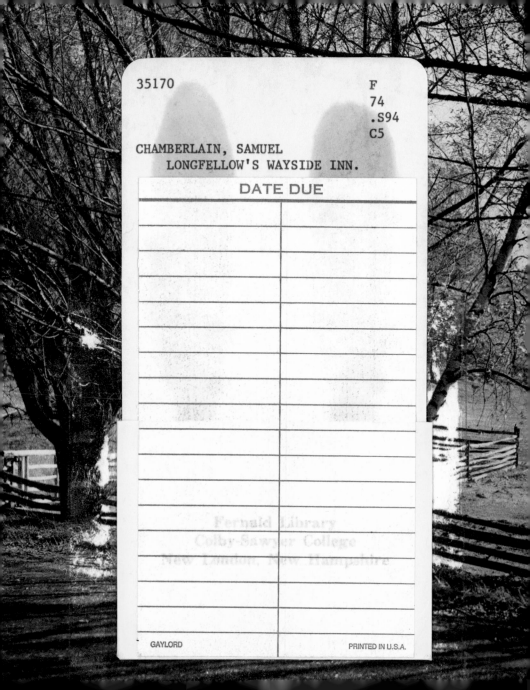